Starting eBay

A Simple and Practical Guide For an eBay Newbie

Publisher's Notes

©2015 Yemisi Oduntan

Contents

Acknowledgments

It has been a journey that could not have been possible without some key people in my life, known and unknown to them for the immense assistance rendered to me.

My husband has always been my main supporter and best critic; my children too have witnessed the many phases of my life and have put up with all my tantrums. I appreciate and thank you all.

Immense gratitude goes to my main inspirer and partner in 'crime' Tele Adewusi; she has continually been a source of support, from the first letter of this publication to the constant nudging at every opportunity. I couldn't have done this without you

Huge thanks to Temi Koleowo of Business Steps 4 Women who sowed the seed of writing in my life at one of her inspirational meet-ups.

About Me

I got the eBay bug from my search for something to occupy my time and possibly earn some extra cash. I was fed up with all the opportunities that required I paid a joining fee, bring one or two people into the business and then after a while it would fizzle out (Does that sound familiar? People would complain about losing money or having a box load of products under the stairs (no names mentioned)!!!!

eBay has exposed me to another side of the online world that I never knew existed. In the early days of embarking on this quest, I felt it was difficult to find all the basic information I needed in one place, and also find practical and realistic guidance that would help manage my expectations. I discovered most books put a lot of emphasis on the huge five or six figure sums that the authors had earned. Don't get me wrong, I admire these people however; I believe success is relative and we all have different goals in our lives and seasons to accomplish them in.

So I thought that I should share my journey by writing this book, to help others who find themselves in the same position as I was starting off selling on eBay. This is a simplistic, practical, realistic guide on the wonderful world of eBay.

Starting eBay - A simple and practical guide for an eBay newbie

WHAT & WHY OF eBay

What is eBay

- eBay was founded in 1995 as an e commerce platform for consumer to consumer and business to consumer buying and selling online. It is based in 30 countries over the world.
- Initially it was just an auction site but the "Buy It Now Option" has now been included and proved quite popular for users.
- There are standard fees for selling transactions on eBay such as listing fees and final value fees that the seller pays.

Why eBay

1. You do not require a huge capital outlay, just looking around the house you can find items to sell that have been gathering dust. Remember one man's junk is another man's treasure!!!!

2. You have what someone else needs and could make good use of. So why not sell it to them and get some cash for it.

3. eBay is simple and user friendly, ideal for anyone who wants to test the waters in online selling.

You will be shocked at what can sell or attempt to be sold on eBay.

In 2005, the original "Hollywood" sign was sold for $450k, the bid started at $300k.

Even a toilet was listed but never reported as sold on eBay, I wonder why!!!!

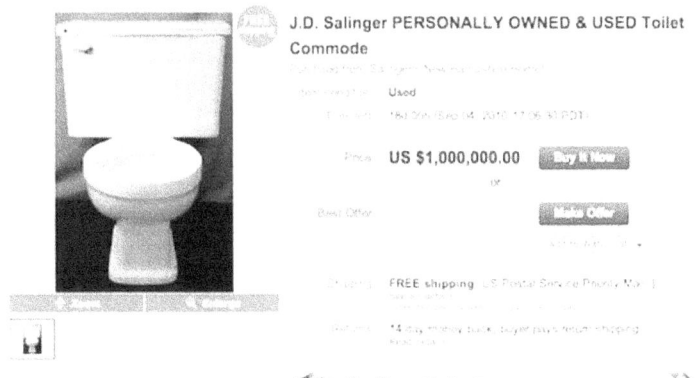

eBay Stars

The wonderful world of eBay has produced quite a few stars making them very rich in the process.

In the UK, the first Brit to make £1million from eBay sales was Mark Radcliffe, a former Tesco shelf-stacker from Stockport, Manchester.

The 35-year-old put aside £200 from his wages to launch First2Save - a one stop eBay shop for mobile phones and technological accessories.

Fifteen years after starting the business from his parents' garden shed, the businessman said he owes everything to the website.

Alison Abruneiras, a mother-of-three from Lincoln, started using eBay to distract herself from the fact that she had cancer. After having to stop work as a nail technician when she was diagnosed with the disease, the 46-year-old became addicted to the online retailer and decided to launch her own shop. Six years after the Nail and Beauty Emporium was started, it now trades with buyers all over the world.

HOW eBay WORKS

The eBay Cycle

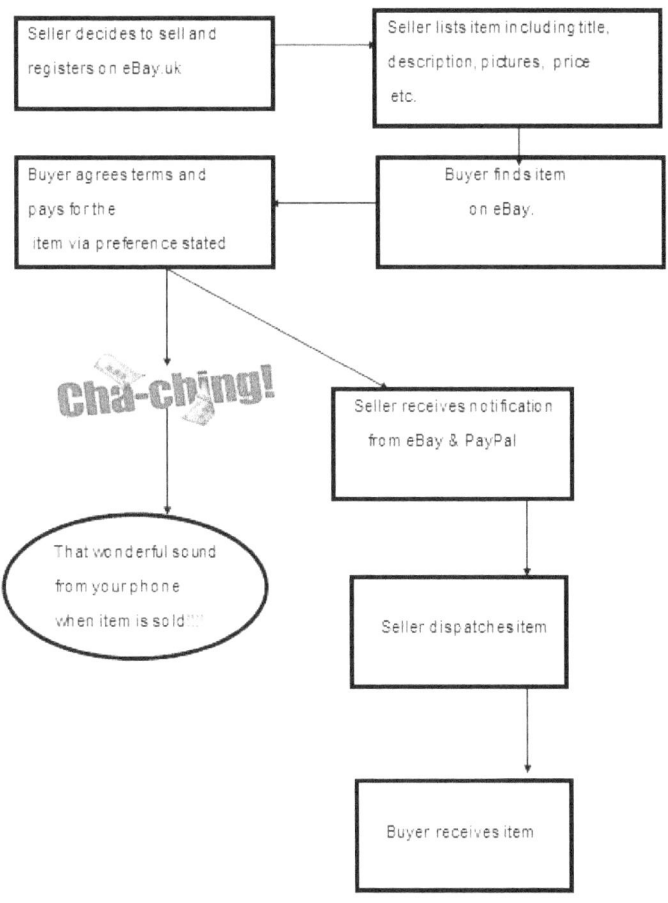

Seller decides to sell and registers on eBay.uk

Seller lists item including title, description, pictures, price etc.

Buyer agrees terms and pays for the item via preference stated

Buyer finds item on eBay.

Cha-ching!

Seller receives notification from eBay & PayPal

That wonderful sound from your phone when item is sold!!!!

Seller dispatches item

Buyer receives item

WHAT CAN I SELL?

This will depend on your reason for starting out on this venture, if it's for a quick spring clean around the house, then that's pretty basic. However, if building a business, then it will be a different ball game entirely and could involve a significant cash injection and a lot more detail.

1. Selling things from around the home that are no longer needed. An article in the Daily Mail of March 2014, revealed study results that showed that a typical home contains an average of £1,650 (£1,000 in 2013) worth of clutter. It is a fact that Britons have a shocking £7.6 billion worth of unused items stashed away in garages and other places in the home.

THINGS I FOUND IN MY CAR WHILE CLEANING

$8 in scratchies

solo jandall

no less than 9 beer bottles

Daphne & Celeste tape

cardboard armour & weapons

Bag covered in badges

Manuscript of the Mangrove

pay & display tickets

a stick

2. Buying smaller quantities of items from clearance stores, markets, charity shops, car boot sales for selling. Depending on what your capital outlay is like.

3. Wholesaling, involves buying goods in bulk and selling individually for a profit. This may require a few hundred pounds, so only advisable if you can afford to tie cash down as it may take some time for you to sell these items so be prepared.

4. There is also a process called Drop shipping, whereby you do not stock the goods, but act

like a middle man between the buyer and seller. This requires a reliable supplier and research. The goods are advertised and once the buyer pays, you then order the goods from the supplier and the supplier ships them directly to the buyer.

HOW TO START

Once you have an idea of what to sell, you will need to open an eBay account. If you have one just for buying you can use the same account. Also if you think you had one and haven't used it in a while, it's best to check with eBay before opening a new one. eBay customer service is quite helpful; they do everything to ensure your requests or questions are resolved. Like most applications nowadays, the Ebay app can be downloaded on to your Smartphone, which makes it easier to use and readily accessible.

- eBay registration would be the first step. It's quite straight forward; all you need is an eBay account. For example in the UK it will be www.eBay.co.uk , or for the U.S it will be www.eBay.com .Always check if your country of residence has an eBay presence.

- eBay requires you have a valid credit or debit card and bank account for some form of identification. A PayPal account is also needed for payments to be received. This is explained later on .

- I recommend you buy from eBay first, to have a better understanding of how the process works. For example you can buy your packaging material such as envelopes or bags, labels tape from eBay. (It could work out much cheaper!!!!)

- For wholesale or other items you will purchase and sell, you need to, decide on a category e.g. Kitchen appliances, jewellery, kids etc.

- If they are used items that were from your home, make sure they are clean, in good condition and well presented. Think about the condition you would like to buy an item in. (Hopefully nice and clean).

- Ask your friends and family if they have anything they no longer require, you will be surprised what they may come up with.

- Carry out some research to see if any similar items are being sold on eBay to give you an idea in terms of pricing, frequency of sales etc.

- Try and list 5 items to start off with, depending on your listing limits with eBay. They usually allow up to 10 items or items up to a designated amount in figures if you are new.

FEEDBACK

There is a popular saying that "Feedback is the breakfast of Champions. eBay takes feedback extremely seriously. As a seller and buyer, you are rated on feedback. Once an item is sold or bought, both parties should leave feedback.

For sellers, feedback is based on communication, description of item dispatch time and postage. Feedback Score is one of the most important pieces of a Feedback Profile. It's the number in brackets next to a member's user ID and it's also located at the top of the member's Feedback Profile.

Buyers review this for credibility to see how the seller has fared in handling transactions. For example if the seller has a lot of returns, it could be a red flag. Below is a snapshot of my feedback profile. Not all buyers leave feedback, but as a seller, make sure once funds have been received, to leave some feedback for the buyer. In the last 12 months I have had one neutral feedback on 175 transactions!!!!

eBay SELLING OPTIONS

Buy It Now

There is an option to list items either as *"Buy It Now"* or at "*Auction"*

'Buy It Now'' gives the buyer the option to buy and pay the fixed price that has been set on your listing immediately by the designated method you have agreed and stated in the listing.

There is also the *"Best Offer"* which can be included as part of the *"Buy It Now Option"*.

Best Offer allows the buyer to offer you a price that they are willing to pay. As a seller you can accept, decline or make a counter offer, the offer is valid for 48 hours.

Best Offer option creates an interest on a listing as buyers tend to look for bargaining power. For example I listed 2 of the jewellery items above with a best offer option of £20, however one was bought at the *"Buy It Now"* price of £27.99 and the other at £20...Not bad right!!!

To avoid getting inundated with offers you can set a cap on a price or that would automatically be declined or accepted by the system.

The upper limit price must be lower than the "Buy It Now" price. If the offer is accepted both parties receive an e mail to confirm the sale and the buyer will be requested to pay.

If the offer is lower, again an e mail is automatically sent to the buyer, declining this offer. For this the seller can send a counter offer or the buyer may submit a higher offer. See the example below.

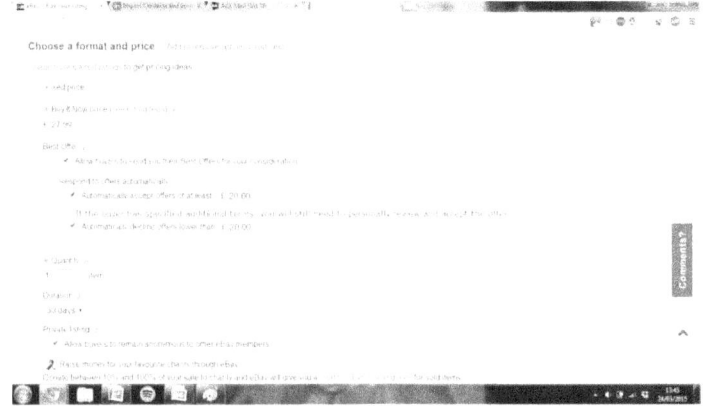

Auction

The auction style format is when the seller lists the item at a starting price and the prospective buyer bids within the duration time, which could be within 7 days.

The buyer enters a maximum price they are willing to pay and eBay automatically manages the bidding by increasing the maximum bid, based on the amount the buyer is has stipulated. Most bids start at 99p, at the end of the auction listing the highest bidder wins.

So for example an item has a current bid for £3.70 and that's the highest bid, another bidder goes for £4.00 and this is the last one before the end of the auction. Ebay contacts the first bidder to state they are outbid and if they don't increase their bid before the auction ends, the winner is the £4.00 bid and will pay the £3.70.

Beware, the buyer will have to pay before the item is despatched, ensure you have received clear payment before you do so!!!!!

Buyers are warned before entering bids that they are sure they want to purchase the item, In rare cases for

example as if an incorrect amount is accidentally entered eBay may retract the bid...

Tips

- Evenings are possibly the best time to end listings; Tuesday, Wednesday, Thursday and Sunday evenings especially. If selling internationally this will need to be tailored due to the difference in time-zones.

- When listing as an auction, make sure the postage costs are covered or you can charge postage separately. For example, if you sell an item you no longer require for 99p and have to pay £4.80 postage out of your own pocket, that's a loss. So the buyer can pay for the postage if it's reasonable and they really want it.

- The item may have only one bidder throughout so ensure your starting price is one you are comfortable selling for.

- It's best to time the auctions, there is no point setting them to end on a Saturday night at 8pm when X Factor is on!!!!!

- Don't end your auctions in the middle of the night when the buyers are tucked up in bed.

Bidders wait till the last minute before they step in.

FEES

You do not want to be out of pocket, so ensure you have an idea of your costs such as eBay Fees, PayPal fees, postage fees and packing costs. Buying an item for £10 and selling for £20, will not make a straight £10 profit. Best use can be made of an EBay calculator. Best use can be made of an eBay calculator, it is a must have and can be found on www.freeeBaycalculator.co.uk.

It automatically calculates your profit after eBay and PayPal fees, once you select the method of selling, the cost price of the item and postage charges

Ebay and PayPal Fees are as follows:

- **Insertion Fees** - For most accounts the first 20 listings are free (check your account terms), then 0.40p each.
- **Final Value Fee** -10% of selling price including postage, using the example above this will be £2 (£20.00*10%). If postage is charged in addition to the sales price for example adding a

£2.80 postage fee to the above, then eBay would charge based on the £22.80

- To receive payment from buyers you need an account with PayPal. www.PayPal.co.uk. PayPal charges a fee for handling the cash paid by the buyer.
- **PayPal Fees**- Fees are between 1.4% and 3.4% of the selling price plus 20p per transaction. The more you sell the less you pay.

PayPal Holds

- If your PayPal account is new, PayPal will want to assure you are a legitimate seller, so once the buyer pays, they will hold the funds received for up to 21 days.
- In that time you would have delivered the goods to the buyer. It is best to provide a tracking number as proof as postage, this shows PayPal you are committed seller.

LISTING YOUR ITEM

Now you have your item, research and check if there are any other sellers on eBay with the same or similar to get an idea of pricing, frequency etc.

If you find a similar item, to save time you can use an existing seller's template and modify it. eBay kindly asks if you have one to sell such as the item, just play by the rules.

Warning- Do not copy the listing in any way shape or form as eBay will be notified immediately. Use your own images, title, and description etc. eBay take copyright as a very serious violation, which could lead to suspension of your account.

When you click on the sell tab (see the far left corner of the eBay heading and welcome with your name on it in the screen shot above) eBay wants to know what you are selling, and asks for a title for your listing. For example if you are selling a dress it will suggest a category you can sell in such as Ladies Clothes etc. It is pretty straight forward just follow through.

Note if you select more than one category you may be charged extra.

Describing your item

The "**Describe**" section in the listing comprises of the **Title of the item, Item Condition and Item Specifics.**

Title of the item

Think like a buyer about how and what would be the best words to describe your item if you were looking to buy it on eBay. If it has a brand name or any other common term use it.

Buyers will use common words to search for. eBay has a search engine that pulls out these words.

For example, a round neck dress could be better described using the size, colour, length and brand. So it will be described as Boohoo Black Dress LBD (Little Black Dress) Knee Length Size 10 could be used.

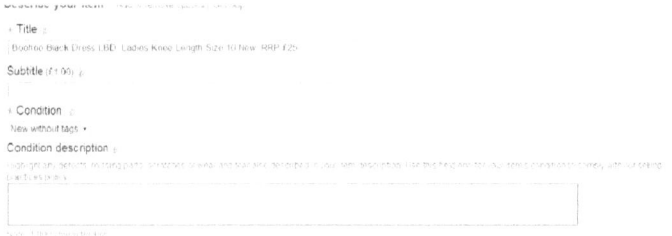

The words should make at least some sense for the buyer to be attracted to the description. Watch out for spelling mistakes, although some words are purposely mi-spelt. For example "Jewellery" and "Jewelery", I guess this is for people who can't be bothered to add the additional "l".

Item Condition

The condition must be as accurate as possible;" New with tags", "New without tags" or "Used". Ensure you are clear in the state of the item being listed.

In the case of any imperfections on the item, it's best to state what exactly it is. For example "slight scratch on the back of bag".

Item Specifics

eBay will prompt you on the specifics in accordance to the category you have chosen. If it's a dress you may be required to include the style, brand, material, length, size type etc. You can adjust these to tailor to your own description.

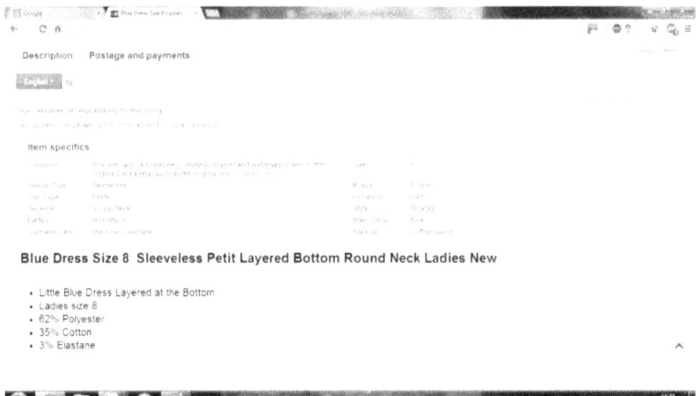

Blue Dress Size 8 Sleeveless Petit Layered Bottom Round Neck Ladies New

- Little Blue Dress Layered at the Bottom
- Ladies size 8
- 62% Polyester
- 35% Cotton
- 3% Elastane

Tips

- Use keywords that will attract buyers, Search for the trends of these words on Google etc.
- Be as accurate as possible; It is the buyers joy when they receive items that are exactly as it was described.

Examples of my feedback with particular reference to description

"great item, as described, perfect, thanks"

"just as described, good quality and very fast FREE delivery, a great seller"

<u>PICTURES, PICTURES, PICTURES!!!!!</u>

Pictures speak louder than words; buyers want to see exactly what they are buying. eBay allows 12 free images of the item you are listing to be uploaded.

Technology has made life so much easier; you don't need a professional camera, simply use your smart phone. Just click upload and you are done!!!

Now which of these pictures would attract you most?

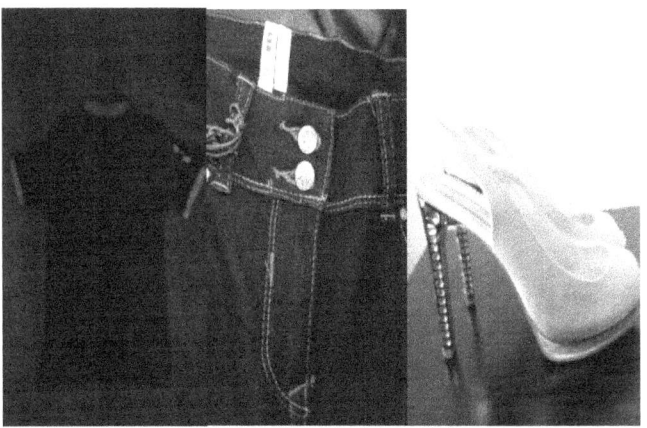

1 2 3

I would say the third one meets all the conditions, it's clear, good lightning etc. Fortunately I did sell the other two items; I guess it wasn't solely due to the quality of the pictures though.

Tips

Make sure there is adequate lighting, dark pictures put buyers off.

- The background is clear, no clutter.
- Take the picture from as many angles as possible e.g. front, back, side, close up etc.
- Use a ruler or a standard object such as a coin to prove the size. Take the pictures beside the measuring tool.
- If there any imperfections, show them in the pictures and ensure this is clearly stated in the description. Buyers don't take kindly to being misled.

PAYMENT

Your payment preferences should be stated on the listing, so the buyer knows the methods you accept. The norm is PayPal.

Some sellers accept credit card or debit card payments through an internet merchant account.

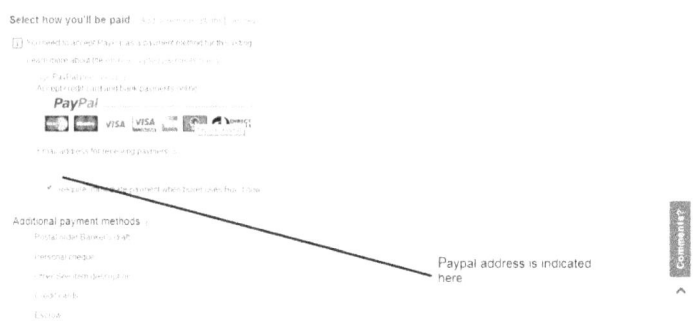

Paypal address is indicated here

PACKAGING

Who doesn't like to receive a nicely wrapped parcel in the post? I certainly do. Your items should be wrapped up and labelled properly. It leaves a lasting impression on a buyer.

You can use brown paper bags or brown paper as alternatives to wrapping as opposed to padded or plastic envelopes which may work out a bit more expensive.

If the items are fragile, ensure they are safely tucked in bubble wrap or air cushions depending on the size. Some business sellers add their personal touch by gift wrapping, etc.

Tips

- Buy your packaging materials such as paper, envelopes, tape etc from eBay or anywhere else in bulk to save a few pounds.
- Ensure the material is strong enough to withstand any condition especially if sending international.

- The cost of the packaging and labour will need to be factored into the pricing especially if you are running a business.

POSTAGE

Postage charges can be factored into the selling price so invariably, it can be stated as "Free Postage" on the listing or the buyer can pay for the postage in addition to the selling price.

You will choose the postal method you prefer "Select Postage" or Offer "Free Postage".

There is an option to send your packages to the UK Shipping Centre and everything else will be taken care of. This called the Global Shipping Programme but will not be addressed in the context of this publication.

Also some sellers may be offered the option to be enrolled in a programme where designated Argos stores are collection points for buyers. This is once they are established and eBay is satisfied with their performance.

Bulky does not necessarily mean more profit; it could be the other way round. Sometimes items can be small and light but do not meet the requirements of a letter and would have to be sent as a package. I have been caught out a few times, and had to pay £2.80 which was not too pleasing to my pocket.

The item below was a typical example of having to pay the price of not checking the postage before listing. I assumed this would be a small parcel as opposed to a letter. However I got a rude awakening on getting to the post office as it did not meet the requirements of a large letter (73p) and so had to be sent for £2.80 .As you can imagine I was not a happy bunny especially as I assumed I would make about £3.42 profit as opposed to £1.35.

<u>Warning</u>

Ensure you send the item to the buyers address listed in PayPal and not one requested by the **buyer**. **There are a few unscrupulous buyers out there who will try and get you to send it elsewhere.** If this is done and any claims are made you are not covered by eBay's Seller Protection.

Tips

- Conduct your research on postage costs before pricing your item. Royal Mail is the standard method, but can be expensive.
- For heavier items check out alternative couriers or even list as "Collect by Buyer"
- Track your parcels so the transaction can be covered by eBay seller protection, especially if it is an expensive item.
- 2nd Class signed for by Royal Mail is usually £3.90 and you are provided with a tracking number to send to the buyer so you know when it was received and who signed for it. There is also compensation cover up to £50,

however conditions by Royal Mail may apply so it's best you check before posting.

- For less expensive items, that are not really worth paying the difference in obtaining signature , you can request proof of postage from the post office, however you may not be covered if the buyer claims it was not received so it's best to weigh the options.

RETURNS & CANCELLATIONS

Many of us have bought items in shops or online, only to discover 'oooppps' it was the wrong size or colour; expect this on eBay as well. In the last month I have had 2 returns as opposed to none in the past 6 months.

eBay makes the process easy with just the click of a button, the funds are refunded via PayPal and the final value fee is credited to your account and will be reflected in your invoice

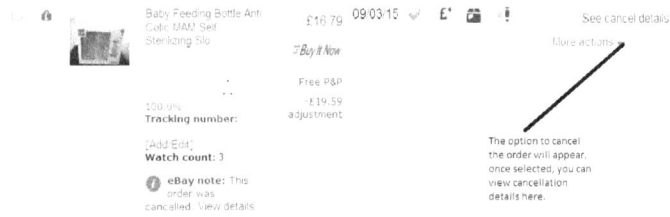

The screen shot above shows one of my returns. It was for an item that I had described with the wrong dimensions even though the actual size was larger than described. The buyer was not happy and felt they had been misled.

Below is an excerpt of our conversations

The bottles arrived today and they are 5.5oz bottles. We have noticed that it says this once in the description but the photos clearly show 9oz bottles including one close up photo of the size on the box. I feel that this has misled us and respectfully ask for a refund of the purchase and postage costs, we will of course, return the bottles to you once you agree"

My reply

"My apologies, this was an error on my part, which I have actually just noticed now. It was not intentional to mislead the buyer (in this case you) in any way shape or form. The description clearly states the condition of the bottles etc a dishonest seller would not do this. I am sorry you feel that you may have been misled.

Kindly return the bottles in the condition you received them; with proof of how much you paid for postage and I will process a refund immediately the package has been received".

After a few days I received the bottles, I had not received the bottles so I sent a gentle note reminding them of my returns policy.

Hi, I have not received the bottles yet. Please bear in mind you have 14 days from the date of receipt to return the item, so I can process the refund.

Buyers Reply

They will be posted today; we have new born twins so it's been hectic.

I eventually received the bottles and processed the refund with an additional amount to cover the postage costs for returning it as it was my mistake...... Customer was happy!!!!

The overall result was that the buyer gave 5 star feedback due to my handling of the situation especially the refund process.

Situations like this can happen, try to stay calm and resolve the issue, communication with the buyer is important. It's best to come to an agreement with the buyer before referring to eBay if you have to. In this case I realised I had under priced the item so on re listing the price has been increased by a few pounds, so it was a blessing in disguise!!!!

Tips

- All communication with the buyer must be through the EBay e mail system, anything outside of this could lead to losing your sellers protection as eBay may not be able to trace if they have to.
- Be polite, professional and as courteous as possible in your communication. Being rude or off key with the buyer could earn bad you feedback, be polite at all times. All you need is a sensitive customer to catch you out on one of those days, so don't let it happen and undo all the good work you have accomplished
- Keep the buyer updated, every step of the way
- eBay can always assist with your return issues if you have any questions or need further guidance.

I hope this has been as helpful as can be and given you possibly enough to at least venture out in to the wonderful world of eBay.

GENERAL EBAY TIPS & NUGGETS

1. If you are just doing this for a hobby or to find some extra cash around the house, start weeding your wardrobe or house for unwanted items. Ask your friends who may have quite a bit of unused items lying around. Remember one man's trash is another man's treasure.

2. Always keep your eyes peeled, there are items everywhere that you can buy and resell at a profit. Check out auction sites, boot sales, charity shops and markets. Stores who are in the process of closing down can also be a good source of items

3. Adhere to your policies, if you say items will be shipped within 2 working days; ensure this is what you do. Buyers are anticipation of their item and expect you to keep to your word. Don't state an item is new when it's not or in working condition. The buyer will have a field day in slapping you down. Be truthful. I once listed a bunch used ties, didn't check properly and assumed they were all from Next, only to find once they had been sold that 3 of them

were from Tesco. I immediately contacted the buyer to explain the situation; she was completely satisfied and asked me to send them to her. She gave me really great feedback in return.

4. Check and review your listings, you may have misspelt a word, stated an incorrect price or selling format. For example listing an item worth £55 for £15, to realise once it's sold that there was an error in the price, could be quite painful.

5. If you need help from eBay you can easily look under the Help & Contact section or call them. The customer service is quite efficient and helpful.

6. Make use of the Community Discussion Boards on eBay, the members are sellers just like you and you can find a lot of information and share experiences.

7. Look out for eBay special promotions, for example they have weekends where you can sign up to list extra items at reduced prices or sometimes for free.

8. List as much as you can manage, you can amend your listing before the sale ends by

tweaking the titles and the prices to attract more views which could result in items being sold.

Have Fun!!!!!!!

REFERENCES

http://www.ebay.co.uk/gds/TOP-5-STRANGEST-THINGS-EVER-SOLD- EBAY/100000011731589g.html

http://www.oddee.com/item_99104.aspx

http://www.dailymail.co.uk/news/article-2641973/End-road-garage-Half-Britains-motorists-use-theirs-store-household-clutter-average-holding-1-650-stuff.html

http://www.dailymail.co.uk/news/article-2729605/The-eBay-millionaires-How-mother-three-Tesco-shelf-stacker-real-life-Del-Boy-fortunes-online-retailer-celebrates-15th-birthday.html#ixzz3V96z5mUZ